PEOPLE SKILLS
FOR
YOUTH PASTORS

**33 Ways to Meet More People and
Make a Bigger Difference in Youth Ministry**

Trevor Hamaker

DOWNLOAD YOUR FREE GIFT

To say thank you for your purchase, I'd like to send you a FREE bonus package. This includes a cheat sheet of the People Skills covered in this book, along with an mp3 coaching lesson on leading volunteers and a 2-week message series you can use with your students.

Download your FREE bonus package today at:

www.betteryouthministry.com/peopleskills

Contents

INTRODUCTION:

WHY YOU SHOULD CARE ABOUT PEOPLE SKILLS

"Our people skills determine our potential success."[1]

-John Maxwell

When you think about the things that determine your potential success, you probably think about IQ, strengths, hard work, genetics, personality type, family background, where you live, schools you attended or experiences you've had.

John Maxwell is one of the world's leading authorities on leadership. When he thinks about the things that determine your potential success, he puts one thing at the top of the list: People Skills.

Think about it:

- Your People Skills determine whether or not people like you.

- Your People Skills determine whether or not people listen to you.

- Your People Skills determine whether or not people want to be around you.

If no one likes you, listens to you, or wants to be around you, how successful do you think you'll be in youth ministry? Not very! That's why it's essential for you to learn about People Skills.

To get started, let's define exactly what we mean by People Skills.

People Skills are a set of skills that allow you to get along with, influence, and communicate with other people in an effective way.

What's shocking to me is that I was *never* taught about People Skills. I don't remember a single class from high school through seminary that taught me how to talk to people, build relationships, and develop influence.

And yet, these skills are a major part of being successful in youth ministry.

People Skills help you stand out in an interview.

People Skills help you make small talk with students.

People Skills help you recruit and retain volunteers.

People Skills help you gain credibility with parents.

People Skills help you get along with other staff members.

People Skills help you distinguish yourself as a leader in your church.

HOW TO WIN FRIENDS AND INFLUENCE PEOPLE

When I was in college, someone gave me a copy of *How to Win Friends and Influence People* by Dale Carnegie. The book was written in 1936, but I went through it as fast as students today go through the *Divergent Trilogy*.

I couldn't believe that no one had told me about that book earlier. The principles were simple, yet profound at the same time.

For example:

- "If you want to gather honey, don't kick over the beehive."

- "Make the other person feel important – and do it sincerely."

- "Talk about your own mistakes before criticizing another person."

People skills were demystified for me when I read that book. It helped me see that those abilities aren't limited to a gifted few; they're available to anyone who is willing to learn the ideas and put them into practice.

Here's a formula you need to highlight:

Better People Skills = Better Youth Ministry

A LITTLE ABOUT ME

I've been involved with youth ministry for over a decade. I've worked at traditional churches and contemporary churches. I've led small youth groups and large student ministries. I've been a volunteer and a staff member.

Additionally, I'm what you would call a "people person." I love meeting new people. I love being around old friends. I love seeing a team of people come together to accomplish a challenging task and have fun while they're doing it.

The RightPath personality assessment classifies me as a "networker." The description says, "Networkers enjoy new people, new situations, and new environments. They use their people skills to build relationships and interact with an ever-widening circle of contacts."

Being a people person has allowed me to meet people, make connections, and grow my influence. There's no doubt that my skills with people have contributed to my success in youth ministry.

But People Skills aren't just for people like me. People Skills are for everyone in youth ministry. No matter who you are, I believe that when your People Skills get better, your ministry will get better.

That's the goal, isn't it?

The point of developing your People Skills is to make your ministry better. People Skills will help you meet more people and make a bigger difference in youth ministry.

There was a time when I tried to one-up people's stories by trying to be the center of attention. I wasn't a good listener. I was abrasive. I was a know-it-all. That's how it goes for networkers like me. I struggled with talking too much, being impulsive, and getting easily distracted.

Just because I liked being around people didn't mean that I was very good at it.

I've worked hard to improve my skills with people. I've read dozens of books on this subject. I've read hundreds of articles and blog posts. I've listened to as many podcasts as I can find. I've come across tips and tricks that have helped me more than I could've imagined. Now, I want to share what I've learned with you.

Whether you naturally connect with people or not, there are some simple ways to help you get the most out of your relationships. That's what this book is about.

I believe the most introverted youth pastor can develop better People Skills. I also believe the most extroverted youth pastor can develop better People Skills. Whichever category you're in, developing better People Skills will you help develop a better youth ministry.

WHAT YOU'LL LEARN

In this book, we'll look at 33 People Skills that will help you meet more people and make a bigger difference.

You'll learn how to:

Create consistently great first impressions.

Make yourself approachable and available to new people.

Dress for success.

Start a conversation with practically anyone.

Double your likeability factor.

Use nonverbal signals to show you're listening.

Turn acquaintances into friends.

Grow your influence so you're seen as a leader.

Own your mistakes to boost your credibility.

Confront people who are causing you problems.

WHAT'S THE POINT?

Again, the point of these skills isn't to make you the most popular person in your church. The point of improving your skills in these areas is to make your ministry better. My experience has taught me that People Skills are vital for doing just that. By the end of this book, I'm sure you'll agree.

READY TO GET STARTED?

Now that you know where we're headed, let's get started...

CHAPTER 1

FIRST IMPRESSIONS
11 WAYS TO STAND OUT IN A CROWD

In the 1990s, Head & Shoulders shampoo commercials reminded us that, "You never get a second chance to make a first impression." They were right. After someone forms an opinion of you, it's very difficult – if not impossible – to change it.

It turns out that first impressions are made faster than you might think. The old-school opinion was that first impressions were formed within one minute of meeting a person. New-school neuroscience, however, suggests that our impressions about people are made in the blink of an eye.

Malcolm Gladwell did extensive research on this phenomenon for his book called *Blink: The Power of Thinking Without Thinking*. He says, "The giant computer that is our unconscious silently crunches all the data it can from the experiences we've had, the people we've met, the lesson we've learned, the books we've read, the movies we've seen, and so on, and it forms an opinion."[2]

I've found that to be true. It's why I can sense when a student is solid or shaky in their faith as soon as I meet them. It's how I know when a parent is friendly before they tell me their name. There's a feel that comes from talking with hundreds of students and parents through the years. No matter what they say, I know what's really going on. So do you.

In the same way, people are forming their own first impressions of you.

You need to be able to stand out in a crowd and create a great first impression. Here are 11 ways that will help you do that:

1. BE POSITIVE

Consider the following two people:

David is upbeat. He sees the best in people, and he doesn't take himself too seriously. Even when things don't go exactly as he would've liked, he remains optimistic that they'll get better.

Mark is easily agitated. He doesn't laugh very often, except when he's making fun of someone else. When things don't go according to plan, he gets upset and focuses on all the reasons it won't work.

Which person would you rather be around?

Of course, the answer is David. He has the qualities of a positive person.

Being positive isn't about wishful thinking or not facing the facts. Positive people can be ruthlessly realistic. The difference comes down to attitude.

Your attitude is your mental outlook. It shapes – and is shaped by – what you think about and expect from other people, yourself, and your circumstances.

Positive people expect the best.

A research study conducted at Harvard University found that 85% of a person's success in life is due to attitude. Only 15% of a person's success comes from their abilities. That means your attitude has a much larger impact on your life and relationships than your intelligence, experience, and talent do.

Your attitude is also important for first impressions. We're attracted to people who are positive. We want to be around people who expect the best. We avoid people who are negative. We don't want to be around people who expect the worst.

Have you heard of Debbie Downer? *Saturday Night Live* created her character for a series of sketches. She always finds a way to make negative comments about whatever is happening. Even at Disney World, Debbie Downer isn't happy. No one wants to be around someone like that.

When people perceive you as a positive person, they'll respond well to you. Your positive attitude will attract them to you and help them to see you in a positive light.

Don't:

Take yourself too seriously.

Do:

Expect the best.

2. STAND UP STRAIGHT

Your body image and body language are both affected by your posture. What does it communicate when you see someone slouching?

Whether the person intends it to or not, they're communicating that they're tired, disengaged, disinterested, closed off, and timid.

Yes, slouching says all of that.

Not only does slouching say those things to other people, but it also sends those signals to the person who is doing the slouching. When you don't pay attention to your posture, you internalize all of those unattractive things. That makes you less likely to meet new people.

On the other hand, when you stand up straight and hold your chin up, you appear more confident and open, which can help you begin to *feel* more confident and open. That will put you in a great position to meet new people.

Instead of being seen as disengaged and sluggish, you'll be seen as engaged and energetic. That can make all the difference when it comes to making a great first impression.

Here's a simple trick to help you stand up straight:

Push your shoulders back about one inch. Nothing huge. Just a little shift.

If you find yourself sitting and talking with people pretty often, the same principle applies. Sit up straight. Here's a simple trick to help you do that:

Sit with your tailbone at the back part of the seat, and put your back flat against the back.

You'll be amazed at what standing up (or sitting up) straight will do for your posture...and your confidence!

Don't:

Slouch.

Do:

Push your shoulders back a little.

3. Put on a Smile

Mother Teresa said, "I will never understand all the good a smile can accomplish." She knew that smiling at someone is a globally recognized way of saying, "I'm glad to see you."

Did you know that smiling is contagious? It really is.

Two studies conducted by researchers at Uppsala University in Sweden found that it's almost impossible to frown when someone smiles at you.[3]

You know how this works if you've ever owned a dog. The dog hears you come home after being at work all day. He's so excited to see you that he practically jumps out of his own skin! You can't help but respond in kind.

The same thing happens with babies. Even grumpy old men smile when they see a baby who is smiling and cooing with joy.

We're happy to be around people who are happy to be around us.

When I was in seminary, I worked in a call center. I was told to smile when I was on the phone because my smile would come through in my voice. They knew what a recent study from Penn State University confirmed: When we smile, we not only appear more likeable and courteous; we're also perceived to be more competent.[4]

The more you smile, the friendlier you appear. So, if you want to make a great first impression, you have to put on a smile.

Don't:

Frown or scowl at people.

Do:

Smile when you meet people.

4. Be Approachable

During the 2015 Super Bowl, Doritos ran a commercial called, "Middle Seat." It showed a man on an airplane that wanted to keep the seat next to him (the middle seat) open. To do that, the man blew his nose, clipped his toenails, and did other things to keep passengers away.

Then an attractive woman boarded the plane. The man caught her attention with a bag of Doritos, only to discover that she was carrying a baby.

In an interview, the commercial's creator said, "My favorite kind of comedy is the sort of comedy where you can look at it and say, "That's funny because it's true. If you've flown, you have probably been in that situation...thinking, 'I hope they do not sit here next to me.'"[5]

How approachable are you?

When people see you at church or around town, are you like the guy trying to keep people out of the middle seat? Or does your demeanor invite them in?

There are three things that hurt your approachability:

1) Being Rushed

When you're moving quickly from one thing to the next, you send the signal that now is not a good time. Replace this with walking slowly through the crowd. Pay attention to each person. Greet people. Smile. Ask for someone's name if you don't know it already.

2) Crossing Your Arms

When you cross your arms, you send the signal that you're defensive and resistant to people. Replace this with keeping your arms at your sides. This communicates that you're open and willing to talk to people.

3) Looking Away

When you're avoiding people, you look away from them. It's like when a student doesn't want to get called on to answer a question. They look away from the teacher. Replace this with keeping your chin up and your eyes forward.

John Maxwell says, "People miss many opportunities for connection and the chance to build deeper relationships because they do not make themselves approachable... It has everything to do with how you conduct yourself and what messages you send to others."[6]

You can't make a great first impression if people don't think you're safe to approach.

Don't:

Push people away.

Do:

Slow down and say hi.

5. DRESS THE PART

When I graduated from high school, I went to Comfort Inn to ask for a summer job. I showed up in a shirt and tie because I knew that would set me apart from other candidates and create a positive first impression. After the manager had hired me, she said that what I wore made a big difference in her choice.

A professor at my seminary was fond of telling us to dress one step above everyone else in the church. He understood the point of a study by Hajo Adam and Adam Galinsky from Northwestern University. They discovered that people who wore a white lab coat were thought to be more professional and given more respect.[7]

To go out and buy a white lab coat would be to miss the point (not to mention weird). The point of the study was to show that our appearance really does affect the way people view us.

We judge books by their covers and people by their appearance. It's just how it is. As soon as you see another person, you form an opinion about them. If they have tattoos on their arms, you form an opinion. Maybe you think that's cool. Maybe you think it's rebellious. Maybe you think it's dumb. Whatever you think, you've formed an opinion.

A few months ago, a guy showed up at my church wearing a tank top, overalls, tuxedo shoes, and a fedora hat. Honestly, I thought to myself, "Wow. He's out of touch." I've gotten to know him in the last couple of weeks, and he's not as far out as I thought he might be. But my first impression of him has stuck with me. I can still hardly take him seriously.

The same thing happens when people meet you.

If you go to the store wearing your pajamas, then people think you're lazy. If your hair is messy, then people think you don't care. If your shirt is wrinkled, then people think you don't know how to do laundry.

That might be the furthest thing from the truth, but it doesn't matter. A person's perception is their reality. That's their opinion of you. It might be wrong, but it's true for them.

Don't:

Dismiss the power of appearance.

Do:

Dress appropriately for the occasion.

6. SHAKE HANDS

When someone reaches out their hand to meet you, grip it firmly and confidently, and shake it. A proper handshake should last for two seconds, which usually works out to two pumps up and down. If it lasts any longer, it will feel like you're holding hands. And that's not okay.

The University of Alabama did a study that found a weak grip means you're anxious, shy, and insecure. They also found that a firm grip means you're self-assured and confident.[8]

When it comes to a handshake, it's important that you get the right grip. Don't be The Dead Fish or The Bone Crusher.

The Dead Fish Handshake is when you place your hand in another person's hand in a limp way. Instead of placing your hand in someone else's, make a concentrated effort to grasp their hand.

The Bone Crusher Handshake is when you grab a person's hand and grip it so hard that it hurts them. As a general rule, you shouldn't grip a person's hand any harder than you would grip a door handle. There's no need for broken fingers during a handshake.

If someone catches you with The Bone Crusher, a good response is, "Wow, that's quite a grip you've got." In most cases, they'll loosen up.

A good handshake is the start of a good relationship. Grip well, and you'll go far.

Don't:

Be a Dead Fish or a Bone Crusher.

Do:

Grasp the other person's hand for 2 seconds.

7. Make Eye Contact

This takes some sensitivity to get right. On the one hand, too much eye contact can be perceived as condescending or intimidating. On the other hand, too little eye contact can be perceived as dishonest or disinterested.

As far back as Cicero (106-43 B.C.), it was recognized that "the eyes are the window to the soul."

More recently, neurological studies have found that eye contact fully activates parts of the brain that allow us to accurately process a person's intentions toward us. No other visual cue does this as powerfully as eye contact. On a side note, that's one of the reasons you don't want to confront someone using a text message or email. A lot can be lost in translation. Even though it can be uncomfortable, it's much better to do it face to face (more on that in Chapter 3).

Eye contact is essential for a good first impression.

So, what's the right amount of eye contact?

As a general rule, if you're familiar with the person, more eye contact is acceptable. If you're not very familiar with the person, soften it up a bit.

One way to get this right is through *mirroring*. When you mirror someone, you pay attention to their tendencies and adjust yours accordingly to get in sync.

The Dale Carnegie Institute advises: "When maintaining normal eye contact, each person looks into the other's eyes and then away again. The speaker checks in visually with the listener, and the listener confirms understanding through meeting the speaker's eyes. This process cycles every few seconds throughout the duration of the conversation."[9]

The right amount of eye contact creates feelings of trust and empathy in the eyes of the person you're meeting. Those feelings are essential for creating a great first impression.

Don't:

Avoid eye contact.

Do:

Use your eyes to communicate trust.

8. LEARN NAMES

One of the sentences I remember from *How to Win Friends and Influence People* said: "Remember that a person's name is to that person the sweetest and most important sound in any language."

I had never thought about that before, and I decided to test out the claim.

When my college baseball team went away to play another school, we would check into a hotel on Friday night, play two games on Saturday, stay that night, and check out on Sunday morning before playing one more game and getting back on the bus to go home.

On the next trip, I met a lady who worked in the breakfast area at our hotel. Her nametag said, Hazel. She told me she was from Germany. I had taken some German classes in high school, so I tried to say a few phrases and she laughed at my broken German. More importantly, I made it a point to remember her name.

When I saw her the next morning, it was time to put the theory to the test. I said, "Good morning Hazel."

You would've thought I'd just given her a $100 bill! She beamed and said, "You remembered my name! You didn't even have to look at my name tag!" She went off with an extra bounce in her step, and I was convinced that Dale Carnegie was right.

Make it a point to learn people's names. Some people say they're just bad with names, but the real reason many people aren't able to learn names very well is that they aren't focused on the person they're talking to.

When someone tells you their name, saying it back to them is a great way to remember it. You could even ask them how to spell it. That will help you remember it too. Then, try to use their name during the conversation 2 or 3 more times. Any more than that can be a little weird.

The best trick I've found when it comes to remembering names is this: Use the person's name when you're saying bye and you'll greatly increase your chance of remembering it the next time you see them.

Don't:

Say you're bad with names.

Do:

Use a person's name.

9. BE REAL

People can tell the difference between sincerity and insincerity. Insincerity pushes people away, but sincerity attracts them to you. We like ourselves better, and other people like us better, when we're authentic and sincere to who we really are.

In his book, *The Likeability Factor*, Tim Sanders identifies four key qualities that can make you more likeable. Those qualities are friendliness, relevance, empathy, and realness.

He says, "There are many definitions of *real*, but in the context of interpersonal relationships, I define it as 'factual and actual'; in human terms, a real person is someone who is genuine, true, and authentic."[10]

One of the ways people seem inauthentic is when they exaggerate. It's easy to do. You're telling a story. You're setting the scene, building it up, adding some color. Next thing you know, the whole thing has grown larger than life.

Everyone embellishes certain details of their stories to heighten the tension or emphasize the main point they want to make. That's fine. The problem is when embellishment turns into exaggeration. That's when you lose credibility, and you're seen as fake.

When I teach students about dating, I tell them, *"Don't act like someone you're not to impress someone you think is hot."* The reason is simple: Even if you're able to start a relationship with that person, it won't last. It will inevitably fail because it was started under false pretenses.

The same thing is true for relationships of any kind. If you want to get started on the right foot, be yourself.

Don't:

Act like someone you're not.

Do:

Be you.

10. BE INTERESTING

In *The Secret Life of Walter Mitty*, Walter Mitty is a guy whose life is predictably boring. He fantasizes about doing great, amazing things, but in reality, he doesn't take risks. He doesn't explore. He plays it safe.

Walter works in the photography department of a print magazine company that is downsizing. With his job on the line, he busts out of his predictable mold. He races across the world doing incredible, adventurous, mind-blowing things in search of a photographer he needs to get in contact with.

Those exploits transform him from a dull, anxious person to a confident, interesting person.

Everyone likes to be around people who have been places and done things that others only talk about. They want to hear all about it. They ask all sorts of questions:

- What was it like?

- What made you decide to do it?

- Who went with you?

- How did it make you feel?

- What was the best part?

- Would you do it again?

People become interested in you when you do interesting things.

Nat Christiana did something so interesting that Taco Bell turned it into a national ad campaign! When the Doritos Locos Taco first came out, he got some of his friends and drove 965 miles to the only place in the country they could get one: Toledo, Ohio.

When they got back home, they had something to talk about. They'd done something interesting. Crazy, yes. But incredibly interesting.

Recently I went to the Tour Championship PGA Tournament. Do I like golf? No. But it was a unique experience that I'll be able to reference for years to come.

Look for ways to get outside of your comfort zone. Whether it's something you've always dreamed of doing or just something you decide in the spur of the moment, doing things makes you more interesting. Plus, you'll always have a story to share. And other people will gladly listen to you talk about it.

You don't have to be the most interesting man in the world, but at least do something that's worth talking about.

Don't:

Be boring.

Do:

Get a life.

11. Clean Up Your Social Media

After someone meets you, one of the first things they do is search for you on social media. Depending on what they find, their opinion of you will either be confirmed or changed.

Here's what I mean:

If you do the things I've talked about so far, a person's first impression of you will be good. However, if they open their Twitter app and find your account filled with rude comments and questionable retweets, then their opinion will change quickly.

On the other hand, if the person you meet thinks you're a nice person, their feeling will be confirmed if they're able to see pictures of you on Instagram serving in the community and cheering for your younger brother's baseball team.

This idea isn't limited to personal relationships. Companies and colleges are now looking at social media accounts to help them get to know a person and decide whether or not he or she is the kind of person they're looking for.

A study conducted by Kaplan Test Prep found that nearly a third of college admissions officers already check applicants' social media profiles, and that number is rising. The study also found that 12% of students were rejected because of content that they posted on social media.[11]

My church was recently hiring for an open position. One candidate had plenty of relevant work experience and a good skill set. But when we looked at his Facebook page, we decided not to hire him. What did we see? We saw that he could be extremely petty and argumentative, especially toward people who had different views than him. His Facebook page cost him a job.

Your social media is like an online resume. People will evaluate your character and competency when they meet you, but they'll confirm their conclusions by cross-checking them against your social media posts and profiles.

Don't:

Post questionable things.

Do:

Treat your profile like a resume.

LAST THOUGHTS ON FIRST IMPRESSIONS

A major part of your life involves meeting new people.

Every person you meet forms an opinion of you in the blink of an eye. That opinion, their first impression, is very hard to change.

No matter how introverted or extroverted you are, these 11 things will help you stand out in a crowd and make a great first impression with everyone you meet.

KEY POINTS FROM THIS CHAPTER

You never get a second chance to make a first impression.

We want to be around people who expect the best.

We avoid people who expect the worst.

Your body image and body language are both affected by your posture.

It's almost impossible to frown when someone smiles at you.

Three things make you appear unapproachable: being rushed, crossing your arms, and looking away.

We judge books by their covers and people by their appearance.

When shaking hands, don't be a Dead Fish or a Bone Crusher.

Pay attention to a person's tendencies and adjust yours accordingly to get in sync.

Make it a point to learn people's names.

Don't let embellishment become exaggeration.

Get outside your comfort zone.

Use social media to present the best version of yourself.

CHAPTER 2

HAVING CONVERSATIONS
11 WAYS TO MAKE AN INSTANT CONNECTION

Now that you've made a great first impression, it's time to talk about conversations.

I developed my conversational skills the most when I was working at Enterprise Rent-a-Car. Enterprise's slogan is, "Pick Enterprise. We'll Pick You Up." If a person didn't have a way to come to the store to pick up their rental car, we would go out and get them. When I wasn't washing cars in my black suit, or trying to sell people car rental insurance they didn't really need, I was picking people up.

The first few times I did it, the rides from the person's house or the repair shop back to the store were awkward and uncomfortable. It's a complete stranger riding beside you in the car. What do you say?

Fortunately, I got better at it. I learned to use the conversational topics and techniques that I'm sharing with you in this chapter. By the time I left Enterprise, picking people up and making conversation with them had become the most enjoyable part of my job.

Whether it's a new student, a parent, or just someone who stopped by the church to ask for help, having a conversation isn't complicated. When you boil it down, it's just talking with another person about what's going on. Someone asks you a question, and you offer an answer. You ask a question, and they give an answer. Questions and answers are the building blocks of good conversations.

Here are 11 ways to have great conversations and make an instant connection with practically anyone:

1. START WITH A COMPLIMENT

In the 1920s, a psychologist named George Crane created the Compliment Club as an assignment for a class he was teaching. Students were instructed to compliment at least three people every day for thirty days.

The results were powerful. One student reported: "I was always shy and tongue-tied but the Compliment Club taught me to forget myself in trying to find good things in the people around me."

Another student said: "People almost always smiled when I paid them a compliment. They were more friendly to me afterwards, and often went out of their way to be nicer."[12]

Compliments don't cost you anything, but they open doors to everything.

John Maxwell is right when he says, "The most fundamental and straightforward way of winning with people is to give them a compliment – a sincere and meaningful word of affirmation."[13]

Here's a typical conversation that I have with a student I've just met on Sunday morning:

Me: Hey, I like that shirt!

Student: Thanks.

Me: Where'd you find that?

Student: At the store.

Me: You must shop at cool places. What's your name?

Do you see how a compliment got the conversation started?

It works with students and adults. It works with people you're meeting for the first time and people you've known for a long time.

Just make sure you mean it. You'll come across as insincere if you go on and on saying flowery, flattering things about someone. The difference is in your sincerity. You have to mean what you say.

Everyone wants to feel good about themselves. When you start a conversation with a compliment, you're helping that person feel special and valuable.

Don't:

Try to flatter people.

Do:

Look for something you like.

2. Be Interested

One of the key principles in *How to Win Friends and Influence People* is, "Become genuinely interested in other people."[14]

Dale Carnegie says, "You can make more friends in two months by becoming interested in other people than you can in two years trying to get other people interested in you."[15]

Think about it:

If I go on and on about what I've done, where I've been, and who I've met, you'll get bored pretty quickly. But if I ask you about the things that you enjoy, you will gladly talk to me for hours.

When you're interested in other people, you encourage them to talk about themselves and their accomplishments.

If someone starts talking about what they did last weekend, a great response is, "Oh Wow! I want to hear more about that." The wrong response would be to draw the attention back to yourself by talking about what *you* did last weekend.

If someone tells you they went to see a new movie that just came out at the theater, a great response is, "What did you think about it?" The wrong response would be to start talking about another movie you saw and what you thought about it.

When a conversation lands on a topic that a person is clearly passionate about, take notice and let them talk. Ask questions that set them up to keep talking.

When the conversation is over, that person's opinion of you will be higher than ever. Why? Because you took an interest in them and let them talk about what they're interested in.

You have to remember that the people you're talking with are far more interested in themselves than they are in you.

Channel your inner Curious George. Because of his curiosity, that little monkey explores new places and discovers new things about the people he's around.

Your curiosity will help others open up to you. There are lots of interesting things you can learn when you learn to listen. If you want to have good conversations, begin to talk about the things that interest other people.

Don't:

Focus on yourself.

Do:

Talk about what interests others.

3. ASK QUESTIONS

Have you ever been in a conversation that was cruising along, and then it crashed? Topics were coming to you, words were flowing with ease, and then…crickets. The air is filled with awkward silence.

Sometimes that lull in the conversation means that you're done for now. Say bye and pick up again later.

But sometimes you don't want to say bye just yet. You want to keep the conversation going. And, of course, there are times when you're stuck in the car with someone and you couldn't say bye even if you wanted to!

What do you do then?

Asking questions is a great way to restart a stalled conversation.

Like I said earlier, conversations are just a series of questions and answers, so the easiest way to get a conversation back on track is to ask another question.

Think about the topics you've talked about already. Is there anything you can ask that goes back and takes one of those topics further?

Maybe the other person said something about a big upset that happened in college football last weekend. You could ask, "What's your favorite college team?" Or, maybe, "Have you ever been to a college football game?"

Those questions can spark all kinds of follow-up questions and answers that will get the conversation moving again.

If you don't want to go back to a topic that you've already talked about, you could always move ahead with, "*So, what do you think about _____?*"

You can fill in that blank with anything you want:

"So, what do you think about the weather lately?"

"So, what do you think about Taylor Swift's new song?"

"So, what do you think about that movie that just came out?"

"So, what do you think about the new restaurant in town?"

You get the point. The question is flexible enough to create a new conversation about whatever topic comes to your mind.

Don't:

Worry about silence.

Do:

Keep it going with a question.

4. LISTEN WELL

How does it make you feel when you're having a conversation with someone and they keep getting distracted?

You know the scene: You're in mid-sentence and they start scrolling through their phone.

Or maybe you're trying to ask their opinion and they're so wrapped up in what's happening across the room that they don't even respond to you.

It's frustrating. It makes you feel like you aren't very important to that person.

The same frustration comes when someone interrupts you or finishes your sentences for you. It's rude.

When you're trying to tell a story and they keep cutting you off, it's like they don't have time for you. Worse, it feels like they don't care about what you're saying. Whether they mean to or not, they're saying that they think their opinion is more important than yours.

That's how someone else feels when you don't listen well. When you're distracted or when you interrupt someone, it sends the message that you don't really care. Whether you mean it or not, it seems like you think your opinion or story is better than the one they have.

That's not the message you want to send. If you want to insert your opinion into the conversation, you should ask, "Would you like to hear what I think?"

It might take some effort on your part, but when someone is talking, focus on keeping your mouth closed and your ears open. Put yourself on mute.

Of course, when someone is talking, you hear what they're saying, but are you really listening? There's a difference.

Hearing doesn't equal listening. When you listen, you're making an effort to connect with what they're saying. You're giving your attention to them. That's rare today. In fact, Tim Sanders goes as far as to say, "I believe attention may well be the newest scarce world resource."[16]

One way you can show someone that you're listening is to nod your head in agreement when they make a point. If the story they share is negative, you could shake your head in disbelief. Those simple actions communicate to the person that they have your attention and you're tracking with what they're saying.

We all want to be heard, respected, and understood. Listening well is a large part of what makes that happen.

Don't:

Get distracted or interrupt.

Do:

Give someone your full attention.

5. FIND COMMON GROUND

When you start a conversation with someone, one of the first things you need to do is find common ground. To do that, you have to be on the lookout for things you have in common with them.

Knowing that someone else has been where you've been, seen what you've seen, felt what you've felt, and experienced what you've experienced forms a bond that is hard to explain. It's just there.

A connection is formed with someone new as soon as you say, "Me too."

I live in Georgia now, but I grew up in Apex, North Carolina. Whenever I find out that someone else is from North Carolina, I feel an instant connection with them.

The same thing happens with the stores you shop at, books you've read, places you've traveled to, hobbies you enjoy, and sports teams you cheer for.

Connection is built on common ground.

Anne Lamott is a writer who says the most powerful sermon in the world consists of two words: Me too.[17]

My wife's dad has Parkinson's Disease. She takes him to the YMCA every Thursday for the Parkinson's Gladiators Class. It's a group of people with the same disease in the same room struggling together through the same exercises with the same goal: to keep Parkinson's from stealing their joy, their health, and their lives. There's a bond in that room that makes everyone stronger.

In your conversations, you want to find out what you have in common with someone and linger there long enough to create a meaningful connection.

Don't:

Focus on your differences.

Do:

Find a way to say, "Me too."

6. Offer Encouragement

In their book, *How Full is Your Bucket,* Tom Rath and Donald Clifton explain, "Everyone has an invisible bucket. We are at our best when our buckets are overflowing – and at our worst when they are empty. Everyone also has an invisible dipper. In each interaction, we can use our dipper either to fill or dip from others' buckets. When we fill others' buckets, we in turn fill our own."[18]

To encourage literally means "to inspire courage." It's not enough to just offer trite platitudes to someone. Those don't actually inspire courage in anyone.

Have you ever received a greeting card from someone who just signed their name under the cheesy, mass-produced message on the inside? Did it encourage you? I doubt it.

When it comes to encouragement, people aren't looking for the professional touch; they're looking for the personal touch. For encouragement to be effective it doesn't have to be eloquent; it has to be personal.

People want to know that *you* believe in *them.*

Tim Elmore offers the image of a hot air balloon for encouragement. He says, "Hot air balloons rise as the burner is released . . . But eventually they begin to fall and need to be re-filled . . . People are like this. They must be consistently encouraged in order to reach their highest potential."[19]

Encouragement is always welcome, but it's especially important after someone gives it their all and falls short. That's when their courage to get up and try again has taken a hit. When you say the right thing at the right time, people will light up and be inspired to keep going.

Unfortunately, a lot of people go away when things don't go their way. But when you encourage someone, you help them see things from a new perspective and believe they can overcome whatever obstacles are in their way.

Don't:

Use empty slogans.

Do:

Inspire courage in others.

7. Point Out Talents

As you're talking with someone, look and listen for something that makes them special or unique. Everyone has *something*. That *something* is called a talent.

Marcus Buckingham says, "Everyone has talents – recurring patterns of thought, feeling, and behavior that can be applied productively. Simply put, everyone can probably do at least one thing better than ten thousand other people."[20]

Everyone you talk to is great at something. It's easier to see in some people than others, but it's there. When you find it, point it out. Call attention to it. Let the person know you see it.

Keep in mind that many people you talk with are filled with self-doubt. They fear they don't measure up. They wonder if they have what it takes. They're looking for validation and affirmation.

George M. Adams said, "I don't care how great, how famous or successful a man or woman may be, each hungers for applause."

If that's true of people who have achieved great things, you can be sure it's true for those of us who are a lot less accomplished.

One of the best ways to create a connection with someone is to let them know you see their talents.

Think about how you feel when your pastor says, "You connect with students better than anyone I've ever met." It makes you feel important and valuable.

When one of your volunteers says, "You did a great job with that message," you feel validated and affirmed.

You feel special and unique when someone points out your talents. Why not help someone else experience that feeling too?

Don't:

Highlight someone's flaws or failures.

Do:

Say what makes them special.

8. FOLLOW THEIR LEAD

Conversations have a flow. There's a back and forth. To connect with someone in conversation and keep things moving, your "back" should match their "forth."

If someone is telling you an exciting story about what they did last weekend, you can match their mood, pace, and volume with your body language and words. That's the flow.

Lean in, raise your eyebrows, smile, nod your head. Say, "Wow! No way! Is that your first time doing that?"

It would be wrong for you to respond with something like, "Well, I'm glad *you* had a good weekend. Mine stunk." That would kill the conversation, and the person would go away to find someone else who will share in their excitement.

Even if you did have a bad weekend, don't share that yet. You'll get your turn. For now, just follow their lead and be excited for them.

On the other hand, not every story is so happy. A student stopped by my office last week to tell me that a friend of his died in a car accident. She had been texting while driving. Clearly my response should be different from the happy conversation.

I put my hand on his shoulder. I shook my head. I kept a straight face. I spoke softly and slowly: "I'm so sorry. How long have you known her?"

This is called *mirroring*. Mirroring is a simple way to help the other person feel like you've heard them. You basically serve as a mirror that reflects what they're saying back to them.

Every conversation is an adventure. You never know which direction the other person will go. Sometimes the tone changes quickly. It's up to you to follow their lead and find the tone that feels appropriate.

Don't:

Forget the flow.

Do:

Act like a mirror.

9. MAKE SMALL TALK

There are times when you find yourself next to people you either don't know at all or don't know very well.

This happens to me when I attend school functions for my kids. Inevitably, I'm standing there next to another kid's dad, waiting for whatever it is to get started. I've seen the guy before. Maybe we've even exchanged the basic pleasantries like, "Which of them is your son?" But that's about it.

We're not friends; we're acquaintances. But if I don't attempt to make some kind of conversation with him, he'll think I'm rude or stuck-up. I don't want that.

The most extreme case is when you're on an airplane. You spend a few hours sitting next to a complete stranger that you'll never see again.

So, what can you say in those situations?

This is the time for *small talk*.

Small talk is a conversation for the sake of conversation. If you're going to be around someone for the next few minutes or several hours, you might as well talk about *something* together. That's the role of small talk.

The best topics are ones that are familiar and easy to talk about. Here are some ideas:

Talk about the weather.

No matter who you're talking with, you have the weather in common. If it's Fall, you could say, "You know, Fall is my favorite time of the year. I just love it. What's your favorite season?"

Talk about current events.

My county hosts an annual fair with rides, crafts, and fried Twinkies. Everyone has an opinion about the fair, so it's an easy topic to talk about. During football season you could talk about fantasy football. Mention something in the local or national news and you'll have plenty to talk about with anyone.

Talk about hobbies.

Everyone has something they like to do. Some people enjoy camping. Other people enjoy cooking or reading. When you ask someone what they enjoy doing, they'll be glad to talk about it. And their answers just might surprise you!

You don't have to make small talk more than what it is. You aren't trying to gain a life-long friend out of it; you're just talking while you pass the time together.

Don't:

Just sit there.

Do:

Break the ice.

10. Let Them Shine

Two big mistakes you can make in conversations are to correct someone in front of other people and to steal the spotlight from them by trying to one-up their story.

Here's what I mean:

Sometimes you find yourself in a conversation with a group of people. One person will make a comment about something, and you know that he's wrong. Maybe he's misled. Maybe he's lying. Maybe he's just coloring in details that didn't happen. Whatever it is, what he's saying is off the mark and you know it.

What do you do? Do you correct them on the spot?

I don't think so. If you do, you'll just embarrass them. Worse, you might make them defensive and resentful. Sometimes you'll even come across as a know-it-all.

Instead of correcting them, I suggest you let the comment go and keep the conversation moving along.

The one exception to this rule is when the person's comment has the potential to create significant confusion or problems for someone else who hears it.

As a pastor, I have a lot of conversations with people about God. The truth is, some people believe some strange things about God. Sometimes they were taught bad theology by a parent or pastor. Other times, they just reached bad conclusions on their own.

When they try to share those strange (unbiblical) beliefs with other people, I feel obligated to say something about it because it can create confusion or problems for other people.

Most of the comments people make aren't on that level. They might not be entirely accurate, but the stakes are low and the outcome doesn't have significant effects. That's when you just bite your tongue. You're better off to let the person save face and feel like they're right.

As for trying to one-up someone's story. Just don't do it. It feels desperate, like you're screaming, "Look at me! Look at me!"

When someone tells a story, let them have the spotlight. You don't need to overshadow them with a more dramatic version of the same thing that happened to you once upon a time.

Don't be the kind of person who walks into a room and says, "Here I am!" Instead, be the kind of person who walks into a room and says, "There you are!"

Don't:

Steal the spotlight from someone.

Do:

Help the other person look good.

11. THINK BEFORE YOU SPEAK

Words have the power to build up or tear down. According to a study by James Pennebaker and Matthias Mehl, people speak around 16,000 words each day. In the study, women spoke an average of 16,215 words, while men averaged 15,669 words.[21] And that doesn't even include text messages, emails, and tweets!

With so many words coming out of our mouths each day, there's a good chance we'll say something that we regret later.

You might say something that crosses the line in a disagreement with your spouse. Maybe you say hurtful things about another youth pastor because you think it'll make you look good in front of your friends. Whatever the reason, when you think back on those moments, you say to yourself, "I wish I hadn't said that."

A sense of satisfaction is at the opposite end of the spectrum from regret. It's the feeling of contentment, a sense of approval, about the things you said. When you think back on those moments, you say to yourself, "I'm glad I said that."

You enjoy that feeling of gladness when you say something that makes someone's day. You find that sense of contentment when you say something that inspires someone to move in the right direction. It feels good when you use your words to make a positive difference.

When it comes to your words, if you want to minimize your regret and maximize your satisfaction, you should think before you speak. This acronym will help you do that:

T   Is it true?

H   Is it helpful?

I   Is it inspiring?

N   Is it necessary?

K   Is it kind?

Together, these questions are a filter that can keep the wrong word from sneaking out. If you can't answer yes to each of these questions, then you should probably keep it to yourself.

Don't:

Say things you'll regret later.

Do:

Use your words wisely.

THE RECIPE FOR RELATIONAL DISASTER

This chapter has been all about conversations. What you say and how you say it matters. Some people never understand that. The ones who do, however, are ready to take their relationships to the next level. They're the ones who will build their influence and make a difference.

It's only fitting to end this chapter with Dale Carnegie's Recipe for Relational Disaster:

"If you want to know how to make people shun you and laugh at you behind your back and even despise you, here is the recipe: Never listen to anyone for long. Talk incessantly about yourself. If you have an idea while the other person is talking, don't wait for him or her to finish: bust right in and interrupt in the middle of a sentence."[22]

KEY POINTS FROM THIS CHAPTER

Questions and answers are the building blocks of good conversations.

Compliments make people feel special and valuable.

People are far more interested in themselves than they are in you.

Asking questions is a great way to restart a stalled conversation.

When you're distracted or when you interrupt someone, it sends the message that you don't really care.

A connection is formed with someone new as soon as you say, "Me too."

Encouragement doesn't have to be eloquent; it has to be personal.

Everyone you talk to is great at something.

In a conversation, your "back" should match the other person's "forth."

Small talk is a conversation for the sake of conversation.

Be the kind of person who walks into a room and says, "There you are!"

It feels good when you use your words to make a positive difference.

CHAPTER 3

BUILDING RELATIONSHIPS
11 WAYS TO GROW YOUR INFLUENCE

You can impress people from a distance, but if you want to influence them, you have to get closer. You have to be open, transparent, and vulnerable. You have to build relationships.

Good relationships don't form overnight. They require a continuous investment of time and effort. When those investments aren't made, the relationship goes away. That's why you've had friends come and go from your life. For whatever reason, one or both of you stopped investing in the relationship.

Time and effort are the prices you have to pay if you want to make a difference in someone's life. It's not easy. That's why so many people today settle for accumulating acquaintances. They're more interested in impressing people than influencing them.

When you build a relationship with someone, you're earning the right to be heard. You're creating credibility and showing them why they should trust and value your opinion out of all the other opinions they hear.

Think about the people whose opinions you value. If you're like me, they're the people you know best. You know that they care about you. You ask for their opinion because you've had a front row seat to their lives and they've earned your respect.

John Maxwell says, "People don't care how much you know until they know how much you care."[23] Taking the time and making an effort to build a relationship communicates to a person, "I care about *you*, not just what you *do*." When someone believes that, they'll listen to what you have to say, and you'll be in a position to make a difference in their life.

Here are 11 ways to build great relationships and grow your influence:

1. BE PATIENT

It takes time to build relationships and grow your influence. Even if you have an instant connection and great chemistry, it still takes awhile for someone to learn they can really trust you.

No one shares their life story on the first date. Instead, they tell you the edited version. They highlight the good parts and cast themselves in the most positive terms they can. It's only later when time has passed, and trust has grown, that they share the not-so-good parts.

Other relationships proceed the same way. You have to be patient with people and give the relationship time to grow. They'll open up when they're ready.

A point of tension in many relationships revolves around personality differences. For example, you might be a go-getter who likes to make things happen. The other person takes their time and likes to talk through all the possibilities before going forward. Your decision-making style is very different, and that can lead to frustration.

Instead of getting frustrated with the other person, you have to practice patience for the sake of the relationship. Give them space to process the options and work through it in their own way. If you don't, then the relationship won't survive, and your influence with that person will dissolve.

Also, it helps to remember that there are many times when other people have to be patient with you. There are times when you change plans. There are times when you're slow to respond. There are times when you say something you would like to take back. When you keep in mind all the ways that other people are patient with you, it helps you remember to be patient with them.

When you involve other people in what you're doing, it might take a little longer to get where you're going, but it's a lot more satisfying when you arrive.

Don't:

Rush relationships.

Do:

Take your time.

2. ADD VALUE

You become valuable to someone when you add value to their life. Instead of focusing on what you can get from another person, focus on the ways you can give to them. To do this well, you need to pay attention to what people value.

A friend of mine is a Florida State football fan. Because we live in Georgia, most of the merchandise available to us is for fans of the University of Georgia and Georgia Tech. A few months ago, I went to Tampa, Florida to see my brother who lives there. While I was there, I saw a Florida State football jersey for kids. I immediately thought of my friend's son.

What did I do? I bought it for him! When I returned home, I gave my friend the jersey for his son. He was so excited and thankful. With that one thoughtful act, I added value to my friend and become more valuable to him at the same time.

Consider all the ways that you can add value to someone else's life. Don't just limit your list to things you can buy. Here are some ideas:

- Offer to help them with a project they're avoiding.

- Send them a link to a funny video they'll appreciate.

- Introduce them to someone you know they'd like to meet.

- Invite them to join you for an experience they'll enjoy.

Dale Carnegie says, "If we want to make friends, let's put ourselves out to do things for other people – things that require time, energy, unselfishness, and thoughtfulness."[24] That's how you add value to someone's life.

My wife has a friend who just became a Christian. The lady is hungry to learn and grow in her newfound faith. My wife meets with her each week to talk about God, the Bible, and life. It doesn't cost any money, but it's incredibly valuable. By giving an hour of her time each week, my wife is adding value, gaining influence, and making a difference.

When you know what people value, you're able to add value in ways they appreciate. Tim Sanders calls this *relevance*. He says, "Relevance is the extent to which the other person connects to your life's interests, wants, and needs."[25]

Natural bonds form when someone sees you as relevant to their life. When that happens, you're on the fast track to influence.

Don't:

Be a taker.

Do:

Be a giver.

3. Earn Trust

Most of us automatically extend a certain amount of trust to everyone we interact with. That's why we're not afraid to drive cars. We trust that other drivers will stay in their lanes and obey the traffic laws.

At restaurants, we don't think twice about handing our credit card to the server. We trust that he isn't writing down the numbers to make online purchases with our information later that night.

We've never met those people, yet we have a degree of trust in them. All over the world, every community depends on that level of basic trust to maintain order.

But when you build a relationship with someone, trust works like a bank account. You take that starting deposit and either build on it or make withdrawals from it.

Michael Abrashoff is a Navy Captain who led the USS *Benfold* to go from one of the most under-performing ships in the fleet to one of the highest. One of the most important things he did was create a climate of trust among the crew.

He says, "Trust is like a bank account – you have to keep making deposits if you want it to grow. On occasion, things will go wrong, and you will have to make a withdrawal. Meanwhile, it is sitting in the bank earning interest."[26]

In your relationships, you make deposits in the trust account when you:

- Tell the truth
- Keep your commitments
- Exceed expectations
- Own your mistakes
- Live with integrity

Withdrawals happen when you:

- Say hurtful things to people or about them
- Show poor judgment
- Underperform
- Pass the blame
- Lose your temper

A relationship usually ends when the trust account goes bankrupt. If you want to make a difference, you have to make consistent deposits that help you earn and keep a person's trust.

Don't:

Make withdrawals.

Do:

Make deposits.

4. Create Memories

An old friend reached out to me on Facebook recently. I got his phone number and gave him a call to catch up. We haven't talked in almost ten years, but we had a great conversation. The thing we kept coming back to was memories that we made together.

You know you're building a good relationship with someone when you can say, "Remember that time when…?"

Creating memories with someone is a great way to form a bond with them.

However, if you want to make memories happen, you have to take the initiative. They don't usually happen on their own. Sure, occasionally you'll see something that you just have to tweet about, and it'll give you a good laugh with someone, but the things that create lasting bonds usually require some planning and forethought to bring together. That's tough because so many of us are already busy and tired with our regularly scheduled activities.

Let me assure you: the extra effort is worth it.

My wife and I take our kids apple picking every October. It's not convenient. The apple orchard is two hours away from our house. Plus, my kids are involved in different activities that are in full swing by October. But we know that the experience is a great memory-maker, so we plan ahead and shift some things around to make it work.

When we're driving home with bags of apples and bottles of cider, we know it was worth it.

Over the last decade, several research studies have found that accumulating experiences is more satisfying and valuable to people than acquiring things. That's why creating memories is so important for building relationships.

But there's a problem. According to a researcher named John McCrone, "The ability to retrieve a memory decreases exponentially unless boosted by artificial aids such as diaries and photographs."[27]

In other words, we move on. We forget about the things we've done. That's why you need to create mementos that enable you (and the rest of the group) to remember and recall the shared experience. It doesn't have to be elaborate or expensive. A t-shirt, coffee mug, or group picture will do the job. Those things become the souvenirs that remind us of places we've been and things we've done.

If you take the time to create a memory with someone, be sure to create a memento too. It'll strengthen your relationship, and every time they see it, they'll remember that time when...

Don't:

Wait to make memories.

Do:

Plan something fun.

5. Celebrate Together

Everyone loves to celebrate when good things happen. Wedding parties are a great example. They're filled with people who are gathered together to celebrate with the bride and groom on their special day.

Graduation parties are another example. When someone finishes school, their friends and family give gifts and send cards to congratulate and celebrate them for a job well done.

Those big celebrations definitely make people feel special. But, there are lots of smaller things that are also worthy of celebration.

- When someone starts a new job, celebrate.

- When someone has an anniversary, celebrate.

- When someone does a remarkable job, celebrate.

- When someone reaches a goal they've been working toward, celebrate.

Unfortunately, many of us let those smaller moments pass by without much fanfare. If we do happen to celebrate someone, it's with a quick text message or

Facebook post on their birthday to let them know we didn't forget about them.

Why don't we celebrate more?

Sometimes we just get busy and forget about it until it's too late. One way to fix that is to schedule the event on the calendar in your phone. Add a reminder a few days before the date, so you'll remember to do something special.

Sometimes we're reluctant to celebrate other people's achievements because of our own jealousy and insecurity. Fight against those feelings. They won't help you build strong relationships, and they'll diminish your influence in the long run.

If you want to build strong relationships and really grow your influence, make celebrating together a priority.

Here are some ideas to help you celebrate someone:

- Tie balloons to their mailbox.
- Give them a gift card to their favorite restaurant.
- Send them a handwritten card.
- Give them their favorite candy.
- Invite them to your house for dinner.
- Decorate their car with streamers and window paint.
- Make a funny trophy or plaque for them.

When my wife and I got married, someone gave us a red plate that says, "You Are Special Today." As the story goes, it was a tradition among early American families to serve someone dinner on a red plate when they deserved special praise or attention. For more than ten years now, we've used that plate to turn ordinary meals into special times of celebration for our friends and family.

Celebration goes hand-in-hand with appreciation. When people are celebrated, they feel appreciated. And when you can make someone feel appreciated, you can be sure that your relationship will grow.

Don't:

Miss the chance to celebrate.

Do:

Make celebration a priority.

6. BELIEVE THE BEST

Relationships are maintained by balancing expectations with reality. If I expect someone to do something and they don't do it, a gap opens between what I expected to happen and what actually happened. How I fill that gap will determine the potential of the relationship going forward.

In a message called, "Trust Versus Suspicion," Andy Stanley says, "Often there are unexplainable gaps between what we expect people to do and what they actually do. We choose what we place in those gaps."

What are the options to place in those gaps?

He says, "We can choose to fill them with trust or suspicion."

With trust, if someone is late to meet you, you assume there must be a good reason. With suspicion, you assume that they're just taking their sweet time and wasting your time.

With trust, if someone doesn't deliver what they said they would, you assume they had the best of intentions, but something got in their way. With suspicion, you assume that they procrastinated, messed around, and ran out of time.

Which one do you think will help you build better relationships: trust or suspicion?

There's no question. Trust is the better option.

You begin to trust other people when you believe the best about them. You choose not to think they're trying to make you look dumb or take advantage of you. You genuinely believe their intentions toward you are good, so you give them the benefit of the doubt when there's a gap between your expectations and reality.

What do you do when they let you down?

There will be times when you believe the best and people let you down. That's just a fact of life. People aren't robots, so you have to allow for human errors, mistakes, and lapses in judgment. That's when forgiveness is necessary.

Forgiveness is choosing not to hold the other person accountable for what they've done. When you forgive, you let them off the hook. You give them another chance. When you believe the best about someone, you believe that they'll learn the lesson from their mistakes and do it differently next time.

Don't:

Fill the gap with suspicion.

Do:

Fill the gap with trust.

7. TAKE RESPONSIBILITY

A teenage girl stopped by my office a few weeks ago because she wanted some relationship advice. She told me about a series of bad boyfriends and broken friendships. After a while, I stopped her and said, "I sense a common denominator in all of these stories."

"What is it," she asked.

"It's you."

To be fair, the fault wasn't all hers. Everyone in her stories could've done things better. But she blamed everyone else for all of her relationship troubles instead of taking responsibility and owning her part of the problem.

In relationships, there will be times when you mess up. There will be times when you get it wrong and let someone else down. When that happens, don't waste your time acting like it didn't happen or giving excuses for why it happened. Own your part.

Admit that you messed up.

Apologize.

Ask for forgiveness.

Then move on.

A study by TARP, Technical Assistance Research Programs, found that 95 percent of customers who have a bad experience at a store would come back and purchase from the store again if they feel like the situation is handled quickly and fairly.

The same thing applies to your relationships. If you make a mistake, don't pass the blame. Own it. Take responsibility. Apologize, and most of the time you'll keep the relationship on solid ground.

In his classic book, *The 7 Habits of Highly Effective People*, Stephen Covey contrasts the Circle of Concern with the Circle of Influence. Things within your Circle of Concern are things that you *can't* do anything about. Things within your Circle of Influence are things that you *can* do something about. This is especially important to remember in relationships.

You get to choose whether or not you take responsibility and apologize. But you don't have the ability to accept your own apology. That's left for the other person to do. They might take the high road of forgiveness, or they could take the low road of bitterness. That choice is theirs to make.

Either way, you are doing the right thing and fulfilling your part of the relationship when you take responsibility for what you do.

Don't:

Pass the blame or make excuses.

Do:

Own your part.

8. SHARE THE CREDIT

There's a difference that I've noticed between football players who score a touchdown and basketball players who score a goal.

When a football player scores, he performs a celebration that calls attention to himself. When a basketball player scores, he immediately points to the player who passed him the ball which led to the score.

John Wooden, the legendary UCLA basketball coach, experienced so much success because he was able to create a sense of unity and team spirit among his players. He taught star players to share the credit and think about "we" before "me."

He says, "A player who is thumping his chest after he makes a basket is acknowledging the wrong person. Thus, I insisted the player who scores give a nod or 'thumb's up' to the teammate who helped – the one who provided the assist."[28]

In twelve years, his teams won ten national championships, including seven in a row.

Let's turn from the basketball court to the boardroom to see another example. Jim Collins, a former Stanford Business School professor, led a team of researchers to identify the factors that allowed some companies to achieve sustained greatness, while other companies in the same industries fell into decline.

His findings are distilled in the book, *Good to Great*. Among the things they found was a principle among Level 5 Leaders (those who possess both personal humility and professional will) that they call *the window and the mirror*.

Collins writes, "Level 5 leaders look out the window to apportion credit to factors outside themselves when things go well (and if they cannot find a specific person or event to give credit to, they credit good luck). At the same time, they look in the mirror to apportion responsibility, never blaming bad luck when things go poorly."[29]

In other words, when things go well, good leaders highlight the contributions made by others. When things don't go well, good leaders take responsibility for the results.

You will experience the same success in your relationships with people if you take the same approach as John Wooden's basketball players and Jim Collins' business leaders. Learn to share the credit. Do it quickly, publicly, privately, and often.

Don't:

Look in the mirror.

Do:

Look out the window.

9. CONFRONT WITH CARE

All relationships move through predictable phases:

1) The Infatuation Phase

Everything is great, and it seems like the other person can do no wrong.

2) The Accommodation Phase

You begin to notice that the other person isn't perfect; they have some annoying habits and character flaws, just like everyone else.

3) The Challenge Phase

Those habits and flaws become more irritating. Differing personalities and desires lead to increased conflict.

4) The Crossroads Phase

You truly know the other person, and must decide if you want to continue the relationship or not.

In every relationship, there will be times when either your feelings or someone else's feelings get hurt. At some point, you'll feel like the others left you out. Maybe another person in your group of friends will feel like their opinion doesn't seem to count. Somebody will say something, and you'll take it the wrong way. Whatever the issue, feelings will get hurt, and people will get frustrated with each other.

What you do with those frustrations and hurt feelings will make or break the relationship going forward. Avoiding the issue and acting like it doesn't exist won't help. It will only hurt more in the long run because nothing will change to make things better.

Instead of avoiding it, you should confront with care. It's the fastest and best way to get back on track.

Notice that I didn't say argue; I said confront. Confronting isn't the same as arguing. The goal of arguing is to win the argument. The goal of confronting is to win the relationship.

Dale Carnegie observes, "Nine times out of ten, an argument ends with each [person] more firmly convinced than ever that he is absolutely right."[30] That's why he counsels, "The only way to get the best of an argument is to avoid it."[31]

Confronting isn't the same as arguing. You *should* avoid arguing; you *shouldn't* avoid confronting.

Before confronting someone, I suggest that you pick your battles wisely. You should be very selective about how much and how often you ask someone to change. If you address too much too quickly, the other person will walk away from the relationship insisting that your demands are too high for them to reach.

Here are five guidelines for confronting with care:

1) Come together

Bring everyone involved together in one place. Sometimes it's just you and another person. Other times there's more. This should not be done through text message or email because too much is left to chance without the advantage of visual cues and body language.

2) Be precise

Avoid generalizations like "you always" and "you never." Also, avoid calling names. Call attention to the situation instead. Don't say, "You're a liar." Instead, say something like, "I feel like you didn't tell me the truth when I asked you about what happened." Calling out their action instead of their character will help them keep from getting defensive. Let the other person know exactly how you feel and why. Talk in terms of your own experience. After all, you don't know what their intentions were; you only know how it made you feel.

Here's a template to use:

"I feel **[insert feeling]**

when you **[insert action]**

because **[insert reason]**."

3) Listen

Ask, "How did that happen?" Then give the other person a chance to explain what happened from their perspective, and why they did what they did. Don't get defensive or rush to judgment. Just listen while they talk. You might not agree with their actions, but at least try to understand their side of the story.

4) Discuss solutions

This is how you keep the situation from happening again. What will be done differently next time? Agree on a few things that each of you could've done differently this time and will do differently next time.

5) Move forward

This process will allow you and the other person to apologize for misunderstandings, help you reach common ground and move forward. Don't hold a grudge or keep bringing the situation up in the future. It's over and done. Move on.

Don't:

Avoid the issue.

Do:

Win the relationship.

10. PRACTICE EMPATHY

The inability to see things from another person's perspective causes a lot of the problems we have in relationships. We need empathy.

Philosopher Roman Krznaric defines empathy as, "the art of stepping imaginatively into the shoes of another person, understanding their feelings and perspectives, and using that understanding to guide your actions."[32]

Empathy is what Henry Ford had in mind when he said, "If there is any one secret of success, it lies in the ability to get the other person's point of view and see things from that person's angle as well as from your own."

Empathy is an intensification of sympathy. Sympathy involves feeling sorry for someone. But you can keep those feelings at arm's length and carry on as usual. Empathy causes you to actually experience what someone else feels. You imagine yourself standing in that person's shoes, embodying the particular situation in which they find themselves.

Think about the last conversation you had that didn't go well. Maybe it was with your senior pastor. He said the youth praise band needs to turn down the volume when they play in the sanctuary on Youth Sunday. You thought that was dumb. You said, "Those old people don't understand what young people want!" That's not a good response.

An empathetic response would try to enter into your senior pastor's shoes. He loves your church. He's trying to lead it through a tough transitional season. He gets emails every week from people who complain about the volume of the music. He's doing the best he can to appease the people who are already there and still reach new people. He has a hard job. If turning down your volume makes his life a little easier, you should do it.

Empathy is powerful because it allows you to meet people where they are, to enter into the situation with them and experience it together. This sense of shared experience creates a deep connection between people.

Tim Sanders says, "Empathy enhances likeability because it delivers many . . . psychological benefits, including a sense of personal worth, clarity, and relief . . . You not only feel appreciated, but validated and less alone."[33]

So, why aren't we more empathetic?

Researcher Daniel Goleman insists, "Self-absorption in all its forms kills empathy . . . When we focus on ourselves, our world contracts as our problems and preoccupations loom large. But when we focus on others, our world expands. Our own problems drift to the periphery of mind and so seem smaller."[34]

In other words, to become more empathetic we need to focus more on others and less on ourselves. That's not easy. That's why you have to practice.

Don't:
Be self-absorbed.

Do:
Get outside yourself.

11. BE A SERVANT

The best way to build relationships and grow your influence is by taking on the role of a servant. The one who serves others will eventually be the one who leads them.

Robert Greenleaf introduced the concept of Servant Leadership in 1970. In an essay entitled, "The Servant Leader," he wrote, "The servant-leader is servant first."

The order of the words is important. A student-athlete is a student first and an athlete second. In the same way, a servant-leader sees their primary role as servant. Because they perform that role with character, conviction, and consistency, they win the admiration of their peers and will be looked at as a leader. The privilege of leading comes as a result of serving.

That means being a servant isn't just a tactic you can apply to your relationships to ultimately get your own way. If you do that, people might go along for a while, but they'll eventually leave you behind when they see you for who you really are.

When you serve others, you convey an attitude of humility. Contrary to some descriptions, humility isn't thinking less of yourself; it's thinking of yourself less.

Humble people are selfless people. They gladly and willingly serve others. They identify and meet the needs of others because they genuinely want to help them succeed and get the most out of life. That's why people love being around people who serve.

Paradoxically, helping others is the surest way to help yourself. That why, long before Robert Greenleaf wrote his article, Jesus told his disciples, "The greatest among you must be a servant" (Matthew 23:11 NLT).

Consider the ways you can serve other people. We've talked about several of them in this section of the book:

- Be patient.
- Add value.
- Build trust.
- Create memories.
- Celebrate together.
- Believe the best.
- Take responsibility.
- Share the credit.
- Confront with care.
- Practice empathy.

These aren't random skills. They're a list of ways you can build relationships and grow your influence by serving the people around you.

Don't:

Think less of yourself.

Do:

Think of yourself less.

WORKING IT OUT

The process of building relationships is like the process of building muscles. When you go to the gym for the first time, you feel sore the next day. You worked out parts of your body that haven't been stretched like that in a long time. But it feels good. You know that's what it takes to be healthy.

You go back. You do it again. It gets easier. Eventually, you start to see results. You don't build big muscles after a week. You don't lose thirty pounds in a month. But you're making progress. You're getting stronger.

That's how it is with relationships. Give it time. Sometimes you'll get it right. Other times you'll get it wrong. Don't quit. Eventually, all of your efforts will pay off. All of those little attempts will add up to make a big difference in your ability to create and maintain healthy, positive relationships. In the end, you'll be glad you did.

KEY POINTS FROM THIS CHAPTER

You can impress people from a distance, but if you want to influence them, you have to get closer.

Time and effort are the prices you have to pay if you want to make a difference in someone's life.

You'll be patient when you remember that there are many times when other people have to be patient with you.

Instead of focusing on what you can get from another person, focus on the ways you can give to them.

When you build a relationship with someone, trust works like a bank account.

If you take the time to create a memory with someone, be sure to create a memento too.

When people are celebrated, they feel appreciated.

Relationships are maintained by balancing expectations with reality.

We can choose to fill the gaps with trust or suspicion.

Own your part of the problem.

Share the credit quickly, publicly, privately, and often.

You *should* avoid arguing; you *shouldn't* avoid confronting.

The inability to see things from another person's perspective causes a lot of the problems we have in relationships.

Humility isn't thinking less of yourself; it's thinking of yourself less.

CHAPTER 4

WRAP UP
A SHORT SUMMARY OF THE BIG IDEAS IN THIS BOOK

If you've gotten this far, then you're ready for success in the days ahead. You're off to great start!

We've covered a lot of ground in this short book, so this chapter will serve as a useful summary of the things we talked about:

FIRST IMPRESSIONS

- Be Positive

- Stand Up Straight

- Put on a Smile

- Be Approachable

- Dress the Part

- Shake Hands

- Make Eye Contact

- Learn Names

- Be Real

- Be Interesting

- Clean Up Your Social Media

HAVING CONVERSATIONS

- Start with a Compliment

- Be Interested

- Ask Questions

- Listen Well

- Find Common Ground

- Offer Encouragement

- Point Out Talents

- Follow Their Lead

- Make Small Talk

- Let Them Shine

- Think Before You Speak

BUILDING RELATIONSHIPS

- Be Patient

- Add Value

- Earn Trust

- Create Memories

- Celebrate Together

- Believe the Best

- Take Responsibility

- Share the Credit

- Confront with Care

- Practice Empathy

- Be a Servant

YOU CAN DO THIS

The tips and techniques in this book are the same ones that I've used for almost fifteen years in youth ministry. Without hesitation, I can say that as my People Skills have gotten better, so has my ministry.

Remember that formula I gave you at the beginning of the book?

Here it is again:

Better People Skills = Better Youth Ministry

You shouldn't try to do everything in this book all at once. You'll get frustrated and give up. You'll think you're just not a "people person."

Instead, I suggest that you pick a few skills and focus on them for a week. Practice them with your students, with your family, and with your coworkers. Then pick a few more skills and focus on those. As time goes by, you'll notice your People Skills getting better and better.

Whether you're an introvert or an extrovert doesn't matter. These skills will help you meet more people and make a bigger difference in youth ministry.

You can do this!

DID YOU ENJOY THIS BOOK?

I want to thank you for purchasing and reading this book. I really hope you got a lot out of it.

Can I ask you to do me a quick favor?

If you enjoyed this book, I would really appreciate a positive review on Amazon. I love getting feedback, and reviews really do make a difference.

I read all of my reviews and would really appreciate your thoughts.

You can also connect with me on Twitter: @betteryouthmin

Thank you!

DOWNLOAD YOUR FREE GIFT

To say thank you for your purchase, I'd like to send you a free bonus package. This includes a cheat sheet of the People Skills covered in this book, along with an mp3 coaching lesson on leading volunteers and a 2-week message series you can use with your students.

Download your free bonus package today at:

www.betteryouthministry.com/peopleskills

LOOKING FOR ONE ON ONE COACHING?

I can help your youth ministry gain momentum and get results.

Here are some of the ways I can help:

RESOURCES

From administrative templates to games to message series, I can connect you with tools that will immediately take your ministry to the next level.

STRATEGY

Some things create more impact and more results than others. I can help you discover what's holding you back and how you can move forward.

VOLUNTEER TRAINING

Your ministry will only be as good as the leaders around you. I can help you recruit, train, and inspire your volunteers.

Personal Development

You are a combination of the books you read, the people you spend time with, and the podcasts you listen to. I can point you in the right direction.

Communication

How you say what you say is important. I can help you craft compelling messages that get students to respond.

Learn more at:

www.betteryouthministry.com/coaching

ABOUT THE AUTHOR

Trevor Hamaker helps youth pastors create momentum, reach students, and grow faith in their ministries. He has over a decade of youth ministry experience, along with degrees in business management, organizational leadership, and religious education.

He has worked on staff at small, traditional churches and large, contemporary churches. Plus, he spent five years working for a multi-million dollar staffing company. Those experiences have given him a unique perspective that can help you get better results in youth ministry.

Find out more at www.betteryouthministry.com.

MORE BOOKS BY TREVOR HAMAKER

Building a Better Youth Ministry: 30 Ways in 30 Days

*Your First 90 Days in a New Youth Ministry:
A Simple Plan for Starting Right*

*Varsity Faith: A Thoughtful, Humble, Intentional, and
Hopeful Option for Christian Students*

*Every Week Matters: Practical Strategies to
Move Your Ministry Forward*

ENDNOTES

1   John Maxwell, *Winning with People: Discover the People Principles That Work for You Every Time* (Nashville, TN: Thomas Nelson, 2004), xiv.

2   Malcolm Gladwell, *Blink: The Power of Thinking Without Thinking* (New York, NY: Little, Brown and Company, 2005), 85.

3   Ulf Dimberg and Sven Soderkvist, "The Voluntary Facial Action Technique: A Method to Test the Facial Feedback Hypothesis," *Journal of Nonverbal Behavior*, March 2011, Volume 35, Issue 1, pp. 17-33. Online: http://link.springer.com/article/10.100 7%2Fs10919-010-0098-6 (accessed 10 August 2015).

4   Ron Gutman, "The Untapped Power of Smiling," *Forbes*. Online: http://www.forbes.com/sites/ ericsavitz/2011/03/22/the-untapped-power-of- smiling/ (accessed 10 August 2015).

5   Sarah Parvini, "Super Bowl Ad 'Middle Seat' Tickles Viewers, Wins Producer $1 Million," *LA Times*. Online: http://www.latimes.com/local/lanow/la-me- ln-super-bowl-commercial-middle-seat-20150202- story.html (accessed 10 August 2015).

6   *Winning with People,* 155.

7   Jordan Gaines Lewis, "Clothes Make the Man – Literally," *Psychology Today.* Online: https://www. psychologytoday.com/blog/brain-babble/201208/ clothes-make-the-man-literally (accessed 10 August 2015).

8   Chris Bryant, "Study Suggests Firm Handshakes and Good Impressions Really Do Go Hand-in-Hand," *Research Magazine.* Online: http://research. ua.edu/2001/08/study-suggests-firm-handshakes-and-good-impressions-really-do-go-hand-in-hand/ (accessed 10 August 2015).

9   Dale Carnegie Institute, *The 5 Essential People Skills: How to Assert Yourself, Listen to Others, and Resolve Conflicts* (New York, NY: Touchstone, 2009), 144.

10   Tim Sanders, *The Likeability Factor: How to Boost Your L-Factor and Achieve Your Life's Dreams* (New York, NY: Three Rivers Press, 2006), 124.

11   Suzanne Shaffer, "How Social Media Can Affect College Admissions," *Teen Life.* Online: https://www. teenlife.com/blogs/social-media-can-affect-col-lege-admissions (accessed 22 September 2015).

12   http://www.complimentclub.com (accessed 10 August 2015)

13   John Maxwell and Les Parrot, *25 Ways to Win with People: How to Make Others Feel Like a Million Bucks* (Nashville, TN: Thomas Nelson, 2005), 34-35.

14 Dale Carnegie, *How to Win Friends and Influence People* (New York, NY: Pocket Books, 1981), 65.

15 *Ibid.*, 54.

16 *The Likeability Factor*, 73.

17 Anne Lamott, quoted in Rob Bell, *Jesus Wants to Save Christians: A Manifesto for the Church in Exile* (Grand Rapids, MI: Zondervan, 2008), 151.

18 Tom Rath and Donald O. Clifton, Ph.D., *How Full is Your Bucket: Positive Strategies for Work and Life* (New York, NY: Gallup Press, 2004), 17-24.

19 Tim Elmore, *Habitudes: Images That Form Leadership Habits and Attitudes*, volume 2 (Atlanta, GA: Growing Leaders, Inc., 2012), 27.

20 Marcus Buckingham and Curt Coffman, *First, Break All the Rules: What the World's Greatest Managers Do Differently* (New York, NY: Simon & Schuster, 1999), 148.

21 Jeanna Bryner, "The Last Word: Men Talk as Much as Women," *Live Science.* Online: http://www.livescience.com/7330-word-men-talk-women.html (accessed 2 October 2015).

22 *How to Win Friends and Influence People*, 93.

23 *Winning with People*, 91.

24 *How to Win Friends and Influence People*, 60.

25 *The Likeability Factor*, 108

26 D. Michael Abrashoff, *It's Your Ship* (New York, NY: Warner Business, 2002), 65.

27 John McCrone quoted in *25 Ways to Win with People*, 30.

28 John Wooden and Steve Jamison, *Wooden on Leadership* (New York, NY: McGraw-Hill, 2005), 128.

29 Jim Collins, *Good to Great: Why Some Companies Make the Leap and Others Don't...* (New York, NY: HarperBusiness, 2001), 35.

30 *How to Win Friends and Influence People*, 117.

31 *Ibid.*, 122.

32 Roman Krznaric, *Empathy: What It Is and How to Get It* (New York, NY: Perigee Books, 2014), x.

33 *The Likeability Factor*, 118.

34 Daniel Goleman, *Social Intelligence: The New Rules of Human Relationships* (New York, NY: Bantam Books, 2005), 54.